LIFE OF A

PLASTIC BOTTLE

by Louise Nelson

BEARPORT
PUBLISHING

Minneapolis, Minnesota

Credits

Front cover – Teerasak Ladnongkhun, franz12, GUNDAM_Ai. 4&5 – DidiPho, Pinglabel. 6&7 – Scisetti Alfio, Parilov, Gaby Fitz, Alexander Knyazhinsky. 8&9 – Gigira, IhorL, Gigira. 9 – photka/Shutterstock. 10&11 – MOHAMED ABDULRAHEEM, Rich Carey. 12&13 – Rawpixel.com, Anna Shkolnaya, MsMaria, Evannovostro. 14&15 – RTimages, Diego Cervo, wavebreakmedia, Rawpixel.com, Karen McFarland. 16&17 – Alba_alioth, Extarz. 18&19 – jantsarik, Douglas Cliff, monticello, kimshanephotos, Pavel Kubarkov, Aphichart Charoenprempri, F8 studio, Seamm. 20&21 – Kristine Rad, Etienne Hartjes, Marija Stepanovic, Olya Detry, Coltty. 21 – Hanna Yandiuk/Shutterstock. 22&23 – Pressmaster, Dan Kosmayer, Huguette Roe, wittaya photo, AlenKadr. Images are courtesy of Shutterstock.com. With thanks to Getty Images, Thinkstock Photo, and iStockphoto.

Library of Congress Cataloging-in-Publication Data

Names: Nelson, Louise, author.
Title: Life of a plastic bottle / by Louise Nelson.
Description: Fusion books. | Minneapolis, Minnesota : Bearport Publishing
  Company, 2023. | Series: Eco journey | Includes index.
Identifiers: LCCN 2021061525 (print) | LCCN 2021061526 (ebook) | ISBN
  9781636919010 (library binding) | ISBN 9781636919065 (paperback) | ISBN
  9781636919119 (ebook)
Subjects: LCSH: Plastic bottles--Recycling--Juvenile literature. |
  Recycling (Waste, etc.)--Juvenile literature. | Recycled
  products--Juvenile literature.
Classification: LCC TD798 .N45 2023 (print) | LCC TD798 (ebook) | DDC
  363.72/88--dc23/eng/20220112
LC record available at https://lccn.loc.gov/2021061525
LC ebook record available at https://lccn.loc.gov/2021061526

For more information, write to Bearport Publishing, 5357 Penn Avenue South, Minneapolis, MN 55419. Printed in the United States of America.

Contents

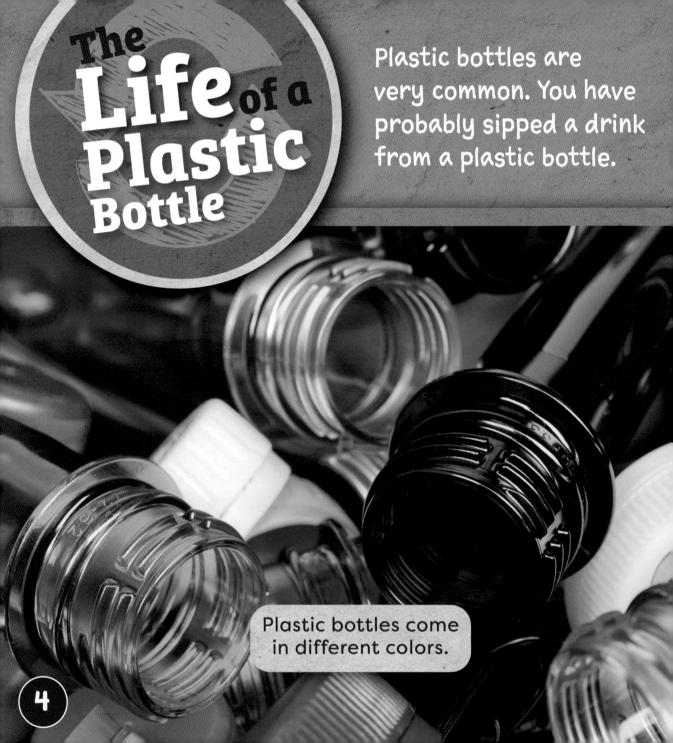

The Life of a Plastic Bottle

Plastic bottles are very common. You have probably sipped a drink from a plastic bottle.

Plastic bottles come in different colors.

But many plastic bottles are made to be used once and then thrown away. They are single-use items.

Do you know what happens to plastic when you're done using it?

5

What Is Plastic?

Plastic is used to make many different things. The plastic in bottles is thin and see-through.

Plastic bottles are easy to bend or crush.

Plastic is made from the **fossil fuels** oil, gas, and coal. They formed underground over millions of years. If we keep using fossil fuels, they'll be all gone.

Coal

Oil

Burning gas

A Single Use

Using fossil fuels to make plastic bottles harms Earth. It can put bad things in the air and water.

Some special plastic water bottles are made to be **reused**.

What should you do with bottles you can't reuse?

Many thin plastic bottles are not made to be reused. They can be hard to keep clean. And the plastic can break easily.

Plastic Pollution

If you throw a plastic bottle in the trash, it will go to a **landfill**. There, the plastic breaks down slowly over hundreds of years. It **pollutes** the land.

Pollution from plastic harms Earth.

Plastic trash also ends up in oceans. It hurts animals and plants.

Ocean animals can get sick and die if they eat plastic.

What Is Recycling?

Luckily, there is another way to get rid of plastic bottles. Instead of throwing a bottle in the trash, you can **recycle** it!

Recycling helps keep plastic out of landfills and oceans.

Recycled plastic is made into something new. It can become a rug, shoes, clothing, and more.

Recycling a Plastic Bottle

Before you recycle a plastic bottle, make sure it's empty and clean. Then, put it in a recycling bin.

Everything in the recycling bin will be taken to a recycling center.

Where can you find a recycling bin?

At home

In parks and other **public** places

At school

15

Becoming New Plastic

At the recycling center, plastic items are washed and **sorted**. They are usually sorted by type or color.

These bottles are all made of the same type of plastic.

Then, the plastic is taken to a factory. The factory **melts** the plastic together and cuts it into small pieces. These pieces are used to make new plastic things.

Pieces of plastic

Trash to Treasure

After a plastic bottle has been recycled, it will become part of a new plastic object. What could be made from of your recycled bottle?

New bottles

A traffic cone

Paving slabs

A plastic pipe

A skateboard

A trash bag

A park bench

A garden hose

Using recycled plastic helps Earth. It is better than making new plastic from fossil fuels.

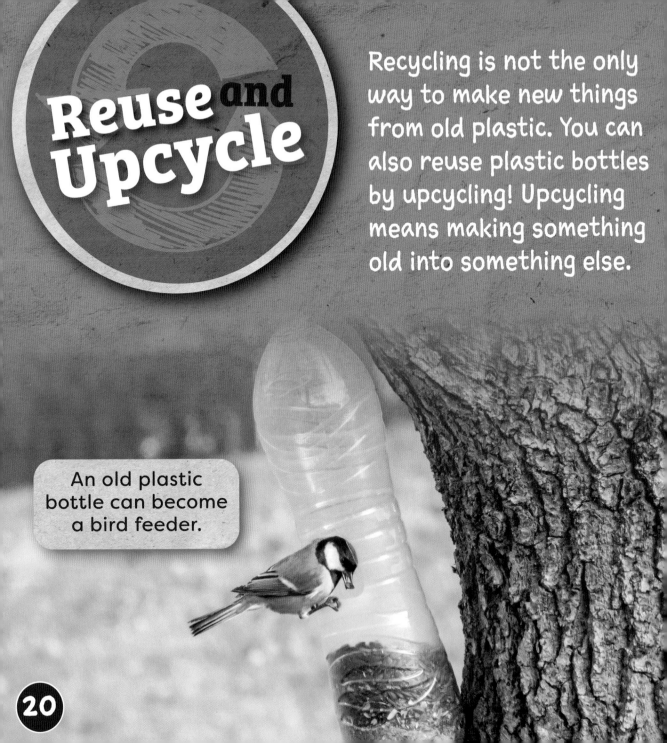

Reuse and Upcycle

Recycling is not the only way to make new things from old plastic. You can also reuse plastic bottles by upcycling! Upcycling means making something old into something else.

An old plastic bottle can become a bird feeder.

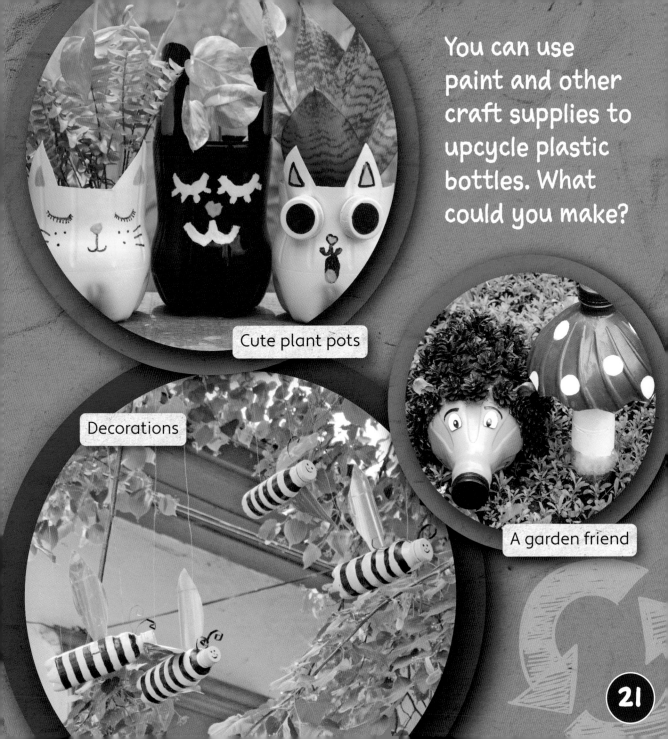

You can use paint and other craft supplies to upcycle plastic bottles. What could you make?

Cute plant pots

Decorations

A garden friend

The Eco Journey of a Plastic Bottle

The plastic is made into bottles or other things.

The plastic is melted to make new plastic.

A bottle is bought and used.

When it's empty, the bottle is put in a recycling bin.

The bottle is taken to a recycling center. It is sorted with other plastic.

Quick Quiz

Can you remember the eco journey of a plastic bottle? Let's see! Look back through the book if you can't remember.

1. What is plastic made from?
a) Trees
b) Fossil fuels
c) Potatoes

2. How long does it take for a plastic bottle to break down in a landfill?
a) One year
b) Hundreds of years
c) Three years

3. How is plastic sorted at a recycling center?
a) By type and color
b) By size
c) Plastic bottles can't be recycled

4. After the recycling center, where does plastic go to be made into new plastic?
a) A landfill
b) A factory
c) An ocean

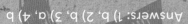

Answers: 1) b, 2) b, 3) a, 4) b

23

Glossary

fossil fuels fuels formed in Earth millions of years ago from buried plants

landfill a large hole in the ground used for dumping garbage

melts turns to liquid by using heat

pollutes makes things dirty in a way that harms Earth

public open to all people in the community

recycle to send something to be sorted and made into new materials

reused used again

sorted put into groups

Index